Introduction

In June 1993 the General Synod of the Church of England received a report from the House of Bishops outlining some preliminary thoughts about 'extended communion'—that is, the practice of distributing bread and wine consecrated in the liturgy of one congregation to another, separate congregation.[1] The report observed that the question had 'received intermittent attention' since the late 1970s,[2] and that the time had come to consider official regulation and authorization of a practice that was already widespread.[3] Eventually, in 2001, the House of Bishops published an official rite for *Public Worship with Communion by Extension*.[4] Thus it now seems that extended communion is an established feature of Anglican worship. The purpose of this essay is to examine the pastoral and theological issues that have led to the authorization of extended communion, and to discuss whether the new liturgy represents an adequate response.

---

1   GS1082 (1993)
2   *Ibid.*, §1
3   *Ibid.*, §6
4   House of Bishops, *Public Worship with Communion by Extension* (Church House Publishing, London, 2001). Relevant reports and draft rites include GSMisc 452, GSMisc 577, GS1230 (1996), GS1230Y (1998), GS1230A (1998), GS1230B (1999), GS1230X (1999), GS1230C (2000)

1

The Origins of the Pastoral Problem

The debate about extended communion arose as a response to a particular pastoral problem: 'the Church of England has increased the sacramental expectations of its laity over the last century…without…being equipped with sufficient stipendiary clergy to meet those expectations'.[5] This imbalance between sacramental expectation and provision of clergy has been addressed in part by introducing new forms of non-stipendiary ministry and by a widespread use of non-parochial and retired priests, drafted in to support parishes that share stipendiary clergy. However, the current rate of retirement and relative lack of ordinands suggests that circumstances are likely to worsen, leading to heightened levels of frustration. Extended communion was introduced to ameliorate this situation, but it remains unclear what the long-term effect will be.

A History of the Eucharist as the Central Act of Anglican Worship
The centrality of the eucharist in Anglican worship probably has no single origin. Some have argued that the composition of the *Book of Common Prayer* itself provides the precedent for a weekly eucharist.[6] Commentators on the BCP agree that the basic pattern underlying its liturgical form combines the offices of Morning and Evening Prayer with a weekly communion. Against common practice, the Reformers emphasized regular communion and denied that the eucharist could be celebrated without the communication of the laity.[7] Despite their best intentions, however, few people desired regular communion, so the eucharist was rarely celebrated. Instead, the regular pattern of Sunday worship comprised matins, litany, and ante-communion, followed later by evensong. Despite the efforts of various churchmen—'high' and 'low'—this persisted almost everywhere until the nineteenth century. So, for example, on Easter Day, 1800, only six people communicated at St. Paul's Cathedral.

The nineteenth century saw a renewed emphasis on the eucharist. While Tractarian concern for the sacrament certainly made an impact in this direction,[8] Horton Davies cautions that it is in fact the evangelicals who 'can rightly be claimed as pioneers in restoring the Sacrament of Holy Communion to its central place in the Anglican cultus'.[9] From early in the century some evangelicals introduced monthly communion, and the number of communicants was often high: attendance at the sacrament was not just a privilege, but a duty.[10] Later, the

5   Colin Buchanan, 'Raising Some Questions' in D Smethurst, *Extended Communion* (Grove Worship Series No.96, 1986), p 18.
6   See P J Jagger, *A History of the Parish and People Movement* (Faith Press, 1978), p 9
7   Cf. rubrics for the *BCP* Holy Communion.
8   See, for example, Tract 26, *Tracts for the Times*, vol.I for 1833-4, (1834)
9   H Davies, *Worship and Theology in England: From Watts and Wesley to Maurice, 1690-1850* (Princeton University Press, 1961), p 223
10   *Ibid.*, pp 223-4

Public Worship with Communion by Extension:

Some Pastoral and Theological Issues

by
Alex Hughes
Assistant Curate, Headington Quarry, Oxford

GROVE BOOKS LIMITED
RIDLEY HALL RD CAMBRIDGE CB3 9HU

Contents

THE COVER PICTURE
is by Peter Ashton

First Impression September 2002
ISSN 0951-2667
ISBN 1 85174 510 6

anglo-catholic 'ritualists' turned their full attention to the eucharist as the central act of Christian worship. Their tendency to emulate Roman Catholic devotion, which had always placed the mass at the centre, made the renewal of a primarily eucharistic piety of paramount importance to them. Moreover, beside theological developments, a pastoral revival and improvements in clerical residence took place during the same period, both of which facilitated a more frequent communion. Thus, during the Victorian age, 'a weekly communion became a feature of almost every parish in the land'.[11] At this stage, however, eucharistic observance was quite unlike the later model of the parish communion, now familiar to almost every member of the Church of England.

Until at least the end of the nineteenth century, communion was still the 'early service', usually held at 8 a.m. as an option for the especially devout. By the turn of the twentieth century some anglo-catholic parishes had introduced an 11 o'clock high mass at which only the priest would communicate, the laity having done so earlier in the day, partly owing to strict fasting rules and partly 'because the polemical spirit of the pioneers insisted that "Mass" was complete without communion, the "sacrifice" being consummated by merely the priest receiving, and this doctrinal truth had to be displayed'.[12]

Pinpointing the start of the parish communion movement is difficult. Various early experiments and episcopal recommendations have all been claimed as the progenitor,[13] and the experience of chaplains serving in the Great War undoubtedly provided grounds for reflection upon the Church's patterns of worship.[14] In 1958, R.H.Martin tried to discover the earliest examples of a parish communion-type service in England. His researches led as far back as 1855 and W J E Bennett's weekly 'High Celebration', introduced at Frome in Somerset—though even Bennett probably had his antecedents.[15] Whatever the case, the picture that emerges is of a number of churchmen all experimenting with new formats for Sunday worship, each of whom placed considerable emphasis on the centrality, accessibility and frequency of the eucharist with general communion. So, for example, introducing the Parish and People Conference of 1962, Henry de Candole looked back upon his own experience as curate in the parish of St.John's, Newcastle-Upon-Tyne, when, in December 1927, 'we transformed a 10 o'clock Children's Eucharist without communicants into a Parish Eucharist, then and ever since habitually known as the "9.15"'.[16] 'The upshot was to bring parents and children together, to bring word and sacrament together, and to form, from pastoral motives, a rite which was intended to lie at the heart of parish life'.[17]

11   Colin Buchanan, *Patterns of Sunday Worship* (Grove Booklet on Ministry and Worship No 9, 1972), p 4
12   *Ibid.*, pp 4-5
13   See H de Candole, 'Twenty-Five Years On' in D M Paton (ed), *The Parish Communion Today: The Report of the 1962 Conferehnce of Parish and People* (SPCK, London, 1962), pp1-5. Cf. P J Jagger, *op cit.*, pp 10ff
14   D Gray, *Earth and Altar*, Alcuin Club Collections, No.68 (Canterbury Press, 1986), pp 35-51
15   R H Martin, 'The Act of Brethren, A History of the Parish Communion Movement', unpublished BD thesis (Queen's, Birmingham)
16   'Twenty-Five Years On' in D M Paton (ed), *op.cit.*, p 1
17   C Buchanan, *The Heart of Sunday Worship* (Grove Worship Series, No 121, 1992), p 10

Over the following decade this pattern of Sunday worship spread. A growing awareness of the continental Liturgical Movement gave it theological reinforcement. The Liturgical Movement began among Roman Catholics on the Continent, notably in the monasteries of Maria Laach in Germany and Mont Cesar at Louvain.[18] One of its primary concerns was for the participation of the laity in the worship of the Church and for their regular communion. Through various contacts abroad, and through the work of theologians like Perret, Heiler and Gavin,[19] a number of key figures in the Church of England came under its influence. Chief among its theological exponents was the group of anglo-catholic clergymen who contributed to A.Gabriel Hebert's collection of essays entitled *The Parish Communion* (1937). Before the publication of this book, Hebert had already introduced some of the Liturgical Movement's ideas in *Liturgy and Society* (1935), and soon afterwards Brother Edward produced *Sunday Morning—The New Way* (1938). Despite the obstacle presented by the Second World War, the movement continued its influence, and was given renewed impetus in the late 1940s with the formation of 'Parish and People', led by de Candole. For years afterwards, Parish and People's eponymously named journal represented the concern for placing the eucharist at the centre of Christian worship. Thus it transpired that the parish communion became almost synonymous with contemporary Church of England worship, to the point that some now see it as an impediment to the Church's mission

> 'It is perhaps the "parish and people movement" which has done more
> than any other single movement to unchurch the people of the United
> Kingdom. It insisted on one sort of service (exclusively the Eucharist) for
> one sort of people at one sort of time.'[20]

However the movement may be criticized, we can assuredly concur with Colin Buchanan's opinion that the Parish Communion 'is the *only* major development of the twentieth century in the pattern of Sunday worship. The Church of England has become universally sacramentalist'.[21]

Before moving on, it is worth noting that Anglicanism's renewed focus on the eucharist as the central, weekly act of worship is part of a pan-denominational interest in the sacrament. A statement made by the World Council of Churches in *Baptism, Eucharist, and Ministry* clearly testifies to this fact:

'As the Eucharist celebrates the resurrection of Christ, it is appropriate that it should take place at least every Sunday. As it is the new sacramental meal of the people of God, every Christian should be encouraged to receive communion frequently.' :[22]

---

18 For a detailed description of the Liturgical Movement's origins see J Fenwick & B Spinks, *Worship in Transition: The Twentieth Century Liturgical Movement* (T&T Clark, Edinburgh, 1995)

19 F Heiler, *The Spirit of Worship* (Hodder & Stoughton, 1926); F Gavin, 'Contemporary Religion in Germany' in *Theology* vol.19, no.113, p 272-282; Perret, 'The Next Hundred Years of Catholic Revival' in *Christendom* (quoted in C Irvine, *Worship, Church and Society* (Canterbury Press, 1993) p 98)

20 M Marshall, *Renewal in Worship*, (Wilton. Conn., 1982; revised and republished as *Glory under your feet: the challenge of catholic renewal today* DLT, London, 1978), p 62

21 Colin Buchanan, *The Heart of Sunday Worship*, p 10

22 World Council of Churches, *Baptism, Eucharist, and Ministry 1982-1990*, Faith and Order Paper 149, (WCC Publications, Geneva, 1990), Eucharist §31

Possible Responses to the Problem

The parish communion movement was largely priest-led, and emerged at a time when the number of vocations was at an unprecedented high. Now that there is a dearth of ministers the expectations fostered by the movement can no longer be fulfilled. Given this problem, four solutions present themselves for consideration. The preferred option must be the ordination of more priests. However, despite a recent increase in the number of vocations, and the introduction of new styles of ministry (e.g. Non-Stipendiary Ministers and Ordained Local Ministers), it seems likely that the shortfall will persist. Another proposal, emanating chiefly from evangelical circles, recommends the authorization of lay people to preside at the eucharist; but this suggestion has failed to win the support of the church, not least because authorized 'lay presidency' is seen as a contradiction in terms: the Church 'authorizes' eucharistic presidency specifically by ordination. It is also worth noting in this respect both that a recent report by the House of Bishops has affirmed a key relationship between the overall presidency of ordained ministers and their specific presidency at the eucharist,[23] and that the Church of England's ecumenical stance upholds the relationship between ordination and eucharistic presidency.[24] A third possibility is to change the pattern of worship prevalent in the Church of England at the moment. However, Synod has expressly stated that parishes accustomed to weekly eucharists cannot be expected to modify their practice.[25] The fourth option, extended communion, increasingly looks like the best solution.

The Historical Background to Extended Communion

The pastoral situation prevailing in the Church of England is not unique. Roman Catholics have been facing the same difficulties in a more acute form for a long time,[26] and certain provinces of the Anglican Communion have likewise found themselves struggling to make sacramental provision for their members. In order to defend the resort to extended communion its advocates have consulted historical precedent. General Synod has also availed itself of this scholarship to justify its authorization of extended communion.[27]

It seems that from an early period in the Church's history pastoral situations arose which entailed the retention of some consecrated bread and wine for communicating those unable to attend the weekly eucharist. The first example of this comes from an account by Justin Martyr, written in the mid-second century, where, at the end of the eucharist, some of the elements were taken by deacons

---

23 House of Bishops, *Eucharistic Presidency*, GS 1248 (CHP, London, 1997)
24 E.g. ARCIC, *The Final Report*, 'The Doctrine of the Ministry' (1982) §12, etc.
25 GS1082, §5
26 In 1988 the Congregation for Divine Worship published a *Directory on Sunday Celebrations in the Absence of a Priest*, which recognizes itself as a response to a *'de facto* situation' ('Introduction'), though admits that it 'should not be regarded as the optimal solution to new difficulties' (§21). The Directory extols the virtue of services of the Word, but claims that these are somehow brought to 'completion' by eucharistic communion: 'In this way the faithful can be nourished by both the word of God and the body of Christ' (§20). For the full text see, 'Directory on Sunday Celebrations in the Absence of a Priest', *Liturgy*, No.13 (Oct-Nov 1988) pp 4-14.
27 GSMisc 452, §3.a.

to communicate those who were absent.[28] At the beginning of the third century Hippolytus describes a kind of 'home communion', in which Christians would take from the weekly celebration sufficient elements to communicate themselves during the week.[29] Cyprian also witnesses to a form of 'home reservation'.[30]

From an early time, then, Christians used the eucharistic elements outside the liturgy. This carried on with very little uniformity throughout the first millennium of Christian history. Around the beginning of the second millennium new extra-liturgical practices began to emerge. As the laity became increasingly alienated from communion, and as theologians began specifically to consider the eucharistic species as *the* locus of Christ's presence in the eucharist, mass became less an action in which to participate and more an object to be seen. The laity went to mass in order to see the host rather than receive the sacrament. This was more or less the pattern that confronted the Reformers, which they tried to subvert. We have already noted that the *Book of Common Prayer* provided for the full round of offices, including holy communion, to be celebrated weekly. The failure of this scheme lay not with Cranmer and the other Reformers, but with the unwillingness of the laity to alter their pattern of worship.

The history of holy communion in England since the Reformation is fairly straightforward. Cranmer produced several orders, culminating in the 1552 Prayer Book when his 'long-standing purpose of producing an explicitly reformed service at last reached its goal'.[31] The so-called 'Black Rubric'—explaining that kneeling reception signified humility and thankfulness, and denying any real and essential presence of Christ in the elements—first made its appearance in this Prayer Book. Furthermore, in response to Gardiner's claim that certain passages in the 1549 Prayer Book supported the doctrine of transubstantiation, Cranmer carefully edited the text to eliminate any ambiguity that might be construed in this direction.[32] Concerning the eucharistic theology of the 1552 Prayer Book, therefore, R.T.Beckwith explains that, 'for Cranmer, as a receptionist, the elements were not sacramental after their sacramental use was over, and he therefore followed Bucer's advice in letting the remains be turned to common purposes again, and Peter Martyr's advice in abolishing extended communion as well as perpetual reservation'.[33] The 1662 Prayer Book largely reproduced Cranmer's earlier work, and certainly maintained his substantially Calvinist view of the eucharist. The rubric to consume any consecrated elements immediately after the rite was not

28   Justin Martyr, *First Apology*, ch.65, in H Bettenson (ed. & tr.), *The Early Christian Fathers* (OUP, 1969) pp 61-2
29   Hippolytus, *Apostolic Tradition*, 36-37. English translation with notes in G J Cuming, *Hippolytus: A Text for Students* (Grove Liturgical Study No.8, 1976)
30   St.Cyprian, *The Lapsed; The Unity of the Catholic Church*, (Newman Press, London, 1957; tr. M Bevenot), p 34. Notice that this primitive communion in a domestic, weekday setting was never expected to undermine or replace the weekly, corporate celebration from which the elements were taken. In other words, the elements reserved at home were the elements over which the communicant had already given thanks in company with the *ekklesia*. Cf. D N Power, *The Eucharistic Mystery: Revitalizing the Tradition* (Gill & Macmillan, Dublin, 1992) p 76
31   R T Beckwith, 'The Anglican Eucharist: From the Reformation to the Restoration' in C Jones *et al* (eds), *The Study of Liturgy* (SPCK, London, 1992 revised edition) p 312
32   Cf. *ibid*, p 312
33   *Ibid.*, p 316

inserted for theological reasons, but to avoid the danger or appearance of irreverence.[34] It is likely, then, that the Reformers' theology would not condone extended communion, and although various alternative liturgies were devised after the legal establishment of the *BCP*,[35] it was not until the nineteenth century that any serious opposition to its rubrics or theology emerged.

The leaders of the Oxford Movement, though deeply concerned to defend a 'high' doctrine of real presence, were neither ceremonial nor liturgical innovators. Hence many tractarians looked askance at the behaviour of the later ritualists. The tendency of some anglo-catholics to look more to Rome than to Canterbury for spiritual and liturgical guidance led to their introducing various practices that had no history in the Church of England. The furore caused by this ritual development is well known. By 1900, the English hierarchy realized that a review of the Church's liturgy and liturgical regulations was necessary to provide for the various parties within the Church; and so began the long, and ultimately doomed, process of Prayer Book revision. In this the attention that the Church gave to questions about reserving the sacrament became dominant.[36] During the years leading up to the Parliamentary votes of 1927-8, a deep divide in the Church emerged over this practice. While reservation was defended largely for purposes of sick-communion, the wise observer could not fail to realise that more basic theological positions—some of which led to such 'Romish' practices as prayer before the Blessed Sacrament and Benediction—were being fought for. The doctrinal cleavage exists even today, despite the recent legalization of reservation (for purposes of communion only, not adoration). The question of extended communion in the Church of England cannot ignore this recent history, and to argue, as General Synod has, that the debate about extended communion does not raise questions about the theology of consecration and real presence looks very much like diplomatic prevarication.[37]

Despite the opposition of the Reformers to any extra-liturgical use of the eucharistic elements, communion extended in cases of pastoral need has proved popular in some places. The evangelical clergyman, David Smethurst, for example, maintains that his experiment in Cumbria 'has proved to be a valuable expression of the ministry of the laity and is now an accepted and much appreciated part of the work and witness of the church in this area',[38] and Phillip Tovey provides many examples of episcopally authorized rites used within the Church long before the publication of *Public Worship with Communion by Extension*.[39] However, while the practice of extended communion has now received official sanction, some serious doubts are expressed about its propriety. A symposium on 'Sunday Worship in the Absence of a Priest' conducted by *Studia Liturgica* in 1996, revealed concerns about extended communion spread over several different countries.[40] Each of the papers comments that, while

34 *Ibid.*, p 316
35 Cf. A Dunstan, 'The Eucharist in Anglicanism after 1662' in C Jones *et al.* (eds), *op.cit.*, pp 318ff
36 Cf. *ibid*, 323
37 GSMisc 452, §3.b
38 D Smethurst, *op.cit.*, p 2
39 P Tovey, *Communion Outside the Eucharist* (Alcuin/GROW Joint Liturgical Study, No.26, 1993) pp19-40. Also, P Tovey, 'The Development of Extended Communion in Anglicanism' in *Studia Liturgica*, vol.30, no.2, pp 226-238
40 *Studia Liturgica*, vol. 26, no.1, (1996)

extended communion originally recommended itself as an acceptable and adequate means of fulfilling the sacramental expectations of congregations deprived of a eucharistic minister, it now seems uncertain whether it succeeds in this role: in fact, it may impair the sacramental imagination and understanding of those experiencing it on a regular basis. Numerous related issues deserve the attention of liturgical scholars, theologians and pastors; however, it is the question whether extended communion achieves its basic goal of sustaining the current eucharistic piety of the Church of England that is the focus of this study.

Public Worship with Communion by Extension

What, then, does the new liturgy for extended communion set out to achieve? In its initial report on extended communion, the House of Bishops observed that some congregations would happily use Morning or Evening Prayer as their primary form of worship, but other congregations 'have grown so accustomed to frequent, indeed weekly, reception of Holy Communion that this provision of some form of non-eucharistic worship on a regular basis would seem strange to them and be unsatisfactory for them'.[41] In a later paper Synod remarked, 'In recent decades worshippers in many parishes have become accustomed to receiving the Holy Communion on every Sunday: it would be unreasonable to oblige them to adopt another form of piety simply because the Church is unwilling to make provision for Extended Communion at a time when fewer ordained priests are available to serve rural cures'.[42] The clear inference here is that Synod expects extended communion to maintain the centrality of the eucharistic life of some churches. So we must ask: how is *Public Worship with Communion by Extension* supposed to meet the 'proper sacramental hopes or expectations' of congregations?[43] In particular, how can we resolve these two statements?

> 'It needs to be clear . . . that the service is *not* a normal and usual celebration of the Eucharist'[44]

> 'It needs to be . . . clear that for those gathered in a particular church on a particular day [for extended communion] there is an offering of worship which should not be perceived as in some sense "second best".'[45]

The problem for Synod is to demonstrate how a service that it emphatically claims is not a eucharist can seem anything but 'second best' by those who maintain a eucharistic piety. Clearly, Synod's view of the eucharist lies at the heart of this. The tension already visible derives from this understanding. On the one hand, Synod assumes that 'receiving the Holy Communion' lies at the heart of the sacrament; on the other hand, it recognizes that a eucharistic celebration requires more than a 'naked distribution' of the elements.[46] It is these two aspects of Synod's theology that need to be explored.

41 GS1082, §5.c.
42 GSMisc 452, §1.b. Later documents extend the provision to cover non-rural parishes.
43 GSMisc 452, §2.c.
44 GS1230Y, §11.a
45 GS1230Y, §11.b
46 Colin Buchanan in D Smethurst, *op.cit.*, p 21

2
Extended Communion and Contemporary Liturgical Principles

As we have seen, implicit in Synod's thinking about extended communion is the view that eucharistic piety revolves around reception of the elements. Not only does this precipitate the Church of England into a debate about the independence of the consecrated elements (an issue to which we shall return later), but it also undermines some key aspects of contemporary eucharistic understanding.

The Unity of the Liturgical Action
Within the Church of England various liturgical principles have emerged which extended communion transgresses. The movement towards the parish communion has a complex history, but underlying its progress are certain basic assumptions, one of which concerns the unity of the eucharistic action. Charles Gore expressed this clearly in response to the growing number of anglo-catholic high masses:

> 'We must not be content with restoring as our chief act of worship a service in which the communion of the people does not form an important part. It cannot be said too strongly that any practice which divorces eucharistic worship and sacrifice from communion, or which rests content at the "high service" with the communion of the priest alone, really represents a seriously defective theology.'[47]

Hebert, who knew Gore's work, continued this vision. In his introductory essay to *The Parish Communion*, he outlined the significance of the whole service (sermon, offertory, communion, etc.) as setting forth 'the whole mystery of redemption…The action is completed in Communion, when that which we have offered is given back to us transformed'.[48] In Hebert's view, communion represents the culmination of a series of actions which, when taken together, are an *anamnesis* ('remembrance') of our redemption. Hence Hebert asks, 'What do Christians do when they meet for worship on the first day of the week?'

> 'They rehearse and set forth the mystery of the divine *agape* whereby man has been redeemed and the redeemed fellowship constituted as the Body of Christ. The central act of their worship must therefore be the act which the Lord instituted on the night that He was betrayed, as the summing up of all His life-work: "Do this in remembrance of Me, do this for my *anamnesis*".'[49]

---

47   C Gore, *The Body of Christ* (Murray, London, 1901) p 276
48   A G Hebert (ed), *The Parish Communion* (SPCK, London,1937) pp 10-11
49   *Ibid.*, p 9

In this *anamnesis* the whole economy of salvation is made present to us, the whole mystery of redemption is set forth objectively. So, Hebert goes on to say:

'Thus in the Liturgy the whole of salvation and the whole nature of the Church are sacramentally set forth. All this is done in the church service sacramentally, that those who have there been brought face to face with the real meaning of things may live their life as men redeemed to God and united in fellowship with one another, and may go about in a world which is out of joint and has lost its true centre, as men who have been called to bear witness to the Truth.' [50]

Notice how important the liturgy is for Hebert. Christ's command to 'Do this in remembrance of me', when obeyed, becomes the ground of every aspect of Christian life: it proclaims the gospel; it reveals the nature of the Church; it enables us to live redeemed lives; it establishes Christian fellowship; and it inspires our mission. For Hebert and his collaborators, it was axiomatic that Christians must be brought 'face to face' with Truth in the eucharist; and this did not refer simply to the act of communion. To demonstrate this, we need only turn to one particular aspect that they championed—the offertory.

From the continental Liturgical Movement, those who promoted the parish communion learnt the importance of lay-participation in worship. Therefore, the offertory—that is, a procession of the gifts of bread and wine to the altar—became known as 'the peoples' liturgy', the ritual action specifically reserved for the laity. Hence it was an important part of the eucharist: it brought the congregation into an intimate relation with the liturgical action. But it was not simply introduced so that the laity could 'play their part' in the eucharist: it had importance as a ritual action in its own right. For through the offertory the Church makes her offering. This idea was closely linked with ideas about eucharistic sacrifice. In fact, the link became so strong that Archbishop Michael Ramsey felt the need to pronounce some cautionary words about its use, urging that we have nothing to offer which has not first been given to us.[51] Notwithstanding Ramsey's concern, however, the offertory continued to find a place in both the popular and educated imagination as one half of an important eucharistic action: we give, then receive our sanctified gifts back. In his book, *Liturgy Coming to Life*, John Robinson stressed the importance of the offertory as the action by which we offer to God our sustenance, our lives, our work and our world.[52] Clearly for him, as for the parish communion leaders, not to participate in this aspect of the liturgy was to miss an important action; and we must therefore ask with Paul Avis, 'What is the theological justification for extended communion, which separates the offering from the reception of the sacrament?'.[53]

---

50 *Ibid.*, p 11
51 A M Ramsey, 'The Parish Communion' in *Durham Essays and Addresses* (SPCK, London, 1956) p 18
52 J A T Robinson, *Liturgy Coming to Life* (Mowbray, London, 1960) pp 37-44
53 P Avis, 'Review Article. Faith and Fantasy in the Countryside' in *Theology*, vol.94, no.758, (March/April, 1991), p 128. It is worth reflecting that Dr Avis writes from a background of ecumenical engagement, in which the eucharist has been a key issue. Ecumenical convergence largely depends on mutual recognition of sacraments, rightly performed and duly administered, and it is hard to see how the rise of extended communion will do anything but complicate the process of mutual acknowledgement.

A distinguished contributor to *The Parish Communion*, Austin Farrer, expressed the symbiotic nature of the whole eucharistic action nicely, saying,

> '[T]he eucharistic action cannot begin till gratitude to God the Father has released it: for it is by thanks for His promise and institution that the Body of Christ is consecrated for our reception, which reception redounds again in eucharist to God.'[54]

We can see, then, how the fathers of the parish communion envisaged the unity of the liturgical action, giving weight to each part. The International Anglican Liturgical Consultation, set up to establish what principles must govern liturgical revision in the Anglican Communion, has given this view contemporary expression. In its statement on the eucharist, IALC-5 said,

> 'We would draw attention to the inter-related character of the traditional parts of the eucharistic prayer inclusive of the opening dialogue . . . thanksgiving to God for his work in creation, the rehearsal of the mighty acts of God in Christ, the institution narrative, the anamnesis, the epiklesis of the Holy Spirit, petitions, and doxology'.[55]

Extended communion does not simply disrupt this united action, it neglects it entirely.

Gregory Dix and the 'Shape of the Liturgy'

Another important figure in the Parish Communion movement was also responsible for introducing an idea that revolutionized liturgical thinking in the Church. Gregory Dix's 'fat green book' brought a new perspective to liturgical study. His basic thesis, that the Church has always and everywhere maintained the same four-action structure in its celebrations of the eucharist—taking, blessing, breaking, sharing—can be found in his contribution to Hebert's volume some nine years before *The Shape of the Liturgy* was published.[56] Since Dix, those responsible for liturgical renewal have been unable to ignore questions of 'shape'.[57] For a long time, his thesis went largely unquestioned and new eucharistic liturgies were deliberately constructed to conform to the four-action shape.[58] Even now that doubts have been raised about Dix's research and conclusions, the question of shape persists. The most recent orders for the eucharist produced by the Liturgical Commission tend to subsume Dix's four actions under two principal actions (blessing and sharing).[59] Nevertheless, the notion that the eucharist comprises several inseparable actions in the one celebration appears to have become universally accepted. The implication of this for our study is obvious: liturgical integrity requires a unity of action, without which the meaning and

---

54 'Eucharist and Church in the New Testament' in A G Hebert (ed), *op.cit.*, p 94
55 Findings of IALC-5: Principles and Recommendations, B4. See D R Holeton (ed), *Renewing the Anglican Eucharist: Findings of IALC-5* (Grove Worship Series No.135, 1996), p 11
56 'The Idea of "The Church" in the Primitive Liturgies' in A G Hebert (ed), *op.cit.*, pp 100-103
57 R Buxton, 'The Shape of the Eucharist: A Survey and Appraisal' in K.Stevenson (ed), *Liturgy Reshaped* (SPCK, 1982) pp 83, 91
58 E.g. Liturgical Commission, *The Alternative Service Book 1980: A Commentary by the Liturgical Commission*, (CIO Publishing, London, 1980), p 58
59 P Bradshaw, 'Gregory Dix' in C.Irvine (ed), *They Shaped our Worship* (SPCK, London, 1998) p 114

intelligibility of the rite is impaired. A R Shands saw this at an early date: 'If the full symbolism of the meal is to come over, we must make clear the "four part shape" of the Eucharist . . . Too often the manner in which we celebrate the Eucharist today obscures the shape'.[60] Similarly, David Tripp sees liturgical shape as providing a sort of narrative structure through which we must pass in order fully to appreciate the eucharist: 'Leaders of worship cannot evade the responsibility for enabling their fellow-worshippers to move together through worship as through a significant and rational process of adoration'.[61] The intrepid leader of liturgical experimentation, Ernest Southcott, also saw the importance of a unified action: 'God does come in a wonderful way to enrich our lives however the Communion is celebrated . . . but surely the fullness of it is brought out if the offertory, the consecration, the Communion, are all seen as the Church acting together.'[62] And throughout his experiments at Clare College, Cambridge, John Robinson emphasized the complete action of the eucharist performed by, and with maximum significance for the whole congregation.[63] John Hibbard brings all these views together in relation to extended communion:

> 'The absence of the fourfold action of the eucharist impoverishes the ritual action of the community. There is no collection and procession of our offerings and gifts of bread and wine to give focus and meaning to our giving. There is no breaking of bread to symbolize our unity in the one bread. There is no receiving from what we brought forth to emphasize the transforming power of God within the assembly...In the distribution of communion outside the eucharist, the community is receiving that which it did not offer, receiving that over which it did not give thanks, and receiving that which it did not break.' [64]

It seems, therefore, that extended communion presents a serious threat to the integrity of the eucharist's shape; and if, as most liturgists believe, certain important—not to say crucial—facets of the eucharist find their expression in different parts of the action, to truncate the liturgy is to damage the sacrament. Communion is only one component action—'the second part of the sacramental action, involving the third and fourth of our Lord's acts'[65]—and it is mistaken to separate it from the action as a whole.

The Eucharist as a Meal

Related to questions about eucharistic shape is the recent 'rediscovery' of the eucharist as a fellowship meal. One of Dix's most famous remarks is that, 'The most important thing we have learned about the liturgy in the past fifty years is that Jesus was a Jew'. The renewal of liturgical scholarship inspired by the

60   A R Shands, *The Liturgical Movement and the Local Church* (SCM, London, 1959) p 105
61   'Shape and Liturgy' in K Stevenson (ed), *op.cit.*, p 80
62   E Southcott, *The Parish Comes Alive* (Mowbray, London, 1956) pp 39-40
63   J A T Robinson, *op.cit.*
64   'Sunday Worship in the Absence of Eucharist' in E Bernstein & M.Connell (eds), *Traditions and Transitions* (Liturgy Training Publications, Chicago,1998) pp 99-100
65   R C D Jasper & P F Bradshaw, *A Companion to the Alternative Service Book* (SPCK, London, 1986) p 231

Liturgical Movement has taken seriously the cultural significance of Jesus' Jewish background, and the result has been to place the institution of the Lord's Supper firmly in the context of Jewish meals.[66]

> 'If all the historical-Jesus study of recent years has not made us certain about details in the Upper Room, it has nonetheless decisively underscored Jesus' wider practice of table-fellowship with disciples and others. We now recognise in this practice a root for the meal-fellowship of early Christianity, which we have come to know as the Lord's Supper.'[67]

If we allow that J Reumann's assessment warns us away from any attempt to investigate the (probably insoluble) questions about the circumstances of the Last Supper, we must nevertheless explore his insight that meal-fellowship lies at the heart of the Christian eucharist. What is the significance of the eucharist as a meal for our understanding of the sacrament and its performance?

Three aspects of the eucharist-as-meal have emerged. First, whatever is said about the particular meal Jesus shared with the disciples in the Upper Room must be placed within a sequence of fellowship-meal experiences during his ministry (and after the resurrection). It is the character of these meals that has drawn most comment from New Testament scholars. Two types of meal are found in the Gospel stories. The first type pictures Jesus flouting convention by eating with sinners and outcasts. This practice, for which he was chastened by the religious authorities, has often been interpreted as a sign of the breadth of God's grace. For the Jew, a shared meal was a sign of solidarity, of fellowship.[68] As part of the eucharist's background, it announces the unity of all Christians— no matter how spiritually or morally impoverished. To gather round the Lord's table is to have *koinonia*. The second type of meal in Jesus' ministry belongs among the miracle stories. The feeding of the multitude is, in fact, the only miracle common to all four Gospels. It seems plain that at the heart of this type of meal lies the idea of God's abundant providence—a theme that John 6 makes explicit. Furthermore, this type of meal was almost certainly identified with the eucharist by the early Church. For example, Mark 6.41 describes how Jesus took, blessed, broke and gave the loaves and fish; and John 6 has generally been seen to have eucharistic resonances.

The second aspect of the eucharist as a meal relates the Christian eucharist to the character of meals in general. The symbolism of communal eating and drinking, along with what is eaten and drunk, has proved to be a rich source of illumination for the eucharist. A more sophisticated view of the way the gospel is mediated through cultural forms has been the source for much critical thinking in this vein. For example, those who, for cultural reasons, believe that the elements used in the eucharist need not be wheat-bread and grape-wine, point to the innate symbolism of food and meals in support of their arguments. On this

66   S J White, *Groundwork of Christian Worship* (Epworth, London, 1997) pp 105ff
67   J Reumann, *The Supper of the Lord* (Fortress, Philadelphia, 1985) p 4
68   B T Lloyd, *Celebrating the Agape Today* (Grove Worship Series, No. 97, 1986) p 4
69   See J-M Ela, *African Cry* (Orbis, New York, 1986) pp 4ff

understanding, bread and wine are meaningful for certain cultural groups—chiefly those of the Mediterranean basin—but are alien in other societies: therefore foods that bear similar meanings to those of the traditional elements should be substituted.[69]

Perhaps the fullest treatment of this aspect of the eucharist is found in David Power's book, *The Eucharistic Mystery*.

'The memory of Christ is appropriated by a community that is brought together around the table on which it has set bread and wine. The symbolism of eating and drinking, or of nourishment, has always served to express the intimacy of communion with Christ that the sacrament offers. What needs stronger elaboration is how the bread and wine in their own selves express human existence, how their change represents the transformation of this existence, and how communion in the blessed flesh and blood of Christ is thus a communion that reaches to the depths of human reality and of Christ's part in it.'[70]

Power goes on to consider the symbolic meal in four aspects. First, he observes how communities express their desires and aspirations by gathering at table:

'At the first level of meaning there is the common significance of bread and wine, expressing the essential urges of hunger and thirst . . . Produced from grain sown in the field and from the grapes of the vine pressed and crushed, they recall the unending struggle between life and death. Signifying nourishment and refreshment, they also call to mind their opposites of famine and drought. Their dependence on seasonal cycles brings humanity into the larger cosmic reality.'[71]

Secondly, Power introduces the relationship between the meal and social and institutional aspects of human life:

'At the second level of signification . . . bread and wine relate to social, economic, and cultural realities. Their production belongs to an intersubjective and organized human society. The needs of the many are met only if there is social cohesion.

'Furthermore, bread blessed at table puts all present in mind of the abundance or want experienced by those who gather . . . [Thus] church gatherings are faced by their ritual with issues of human need and justice.'[72]

The third feature of the meal involves sharing in a community of mutual service and non-discrimination:

'Coming to the significance drawn from the nature of the community that gathers, the sharing of bread and wine takes on the characteristics of Christian assembly. It belongs to the bonding of believers in common identity, in mutual service, in charity, and in hope.'[73]

70   D M Power, *op.cit.*, p 295
71   *Ibid.*, p 295
72   *Ibid.*, p 295
73   *Ibid.*, p 295

His final observation is that, because of the blessing, gathering at table becomes the action through which the death and resurrection of Christ are proclaimed and he himself is present at the table as servant and Lord, 'transforming the manner of their presence in the world in which they live and to which they give shape and offering his own self as life's nourishment'.

> '[All] the innate meaning of food and drink . . . is taken up into the eschatological promise of the passion narrative, the images of the table playing with the remembrance of the passion . . .
>
> 'Being one with the earth, being in the world, being together as a community that hopes, are affirmed but transformed by the memory of Christ and the blessing that it evokes.'[74]

Each of Power's four categories emphasizes the social or communal nature of the eucharistic meal: it has an outward-looking perspective, which is hallowed by its connection with the *anamnesis* of Christ's death and resurrection. The vision of a community gathering for a meal, bringing food and drink as symbols of their common life in the world is shattered by extended communion. In extended communion, not only has the congregation not gathered around the table upon which they have laid gifts representing their own lives, but the emphasis in eating and drinking is different. There is a latent individualism involved in 'making my communion'. Robinson picks up this theme in *Liturgy Coming to Life*. Though committed to the parish eucharist, he criticizes the modern call to regular communion as if it were a private devotional exercise. He stresses that we come not just to feed on the body of Christ but to be created the body of Christ. Robinson regrets that preparation for communion—especially confirmation training—tends to prepare us for 'making our communion', rather than for the idea that in the eucharist the congregation is made Christ's body. He protests therefore, saying 'Communion is not something "I" can "make" but only "we" can "do".'[75]

The final aspect of the eucharistic meal is its eschatological perspective. At the eucharist, the Church-militant is united with the Church-triumphant in a foretaste of the feast of the Kingdom. This is particularly important for Paul McPartlan in his exposition of eucharistic ecclesiology according to Henri de Lubac and John Zizioulas. McPartlan explains that in the eucharist the Church is made or created— hence the title of his book, *The Eucharist Makes the Church*.[76] The Church, as the body of Christ, exists in its fullness only at the eschaton, when all believers are united in the eternal Kingdom of God. Until this consummation, the Church exists on earth only as it is in communion with the eschatological body of Christ—a sort of 'proleptic existence'. This reality is founded upon our sharing in the eucharist, the sacrament of the body of Christ. Now although McPartlan does not discuss the question of liturgical integrity in relation to the eucharist, there are certain aspects of the liturgy that are designed to communicate the idea that participants

---

74   *Ibid.*, pp 295-6
75   J A T Robinson, *op.cit.*, pp 27-8
76   The title is a maxim coined by Henri de Lubac.

join in the heavenly worship of the Church-triumphant. Perhaps the most obvious example is the *Sanctus* (one of the few places where the whole congregation speak), in which we are invited to join our praises with those of the heavenly host. It seems plain that a 'naked distribution' of the elements completely fails to express the sense of corporateness, both in the present and eschatologically, which McPartlan sees as essential to the eucharist.

Before moving to the next section of our discussion, another, slightly unusual, aspect of the eucharist as a meal has emerged recently. In 1994, G Lapointe wrote an article about televised Sunday mass in French Canada.[77] To the question, 'Is it a eucharist that *really* takes place for the viewer?' he answers 'No', because 'mass has its own conditions, its own symbolic space with its own laws of communication, which govern the interactions among believers *around the table* . . . The birthplace of the Christian eucharist determines a certain type of communication, of which we should never lose sight'.[78] His argument is that the early Church found expression of its faith in a domestic setting, sharing bread and wine, but that over many years, this original setting became obscured so that, 'The eucharist progressively lost its supper dimension and, of course, its sharing dimension, to become a *distribution of communion*' and ultimately a 'eucharist-spectacle'.[79] Lapointe's observation that 'the church was born *around a table*, in a meal setting',[80] and that this sets up certain boundaries for its legitimate celebration, has clear implications for our study. There is, perhaps, an echo of this concern in Paul Gibson's and Clay Morris' article, 'Preserving Unity at Large Celebrations of the Eucharist' in which they try to answer the question, 'How far away from the celebration do you have to be before the unity of elements and action is broken?' Their response is that 'the people must be fed from bread and wine over which the presider has given visible thanks'.[81] In both this article and Lapointe's, the underlying concern is that the character of the eucharist as a meal in which bread and wine are shared must always be explicit.

Although we could say more about the eucharist as a meal, it is already clear that this aspect of its celebration must be transparent. While it might, of course, be argued that simply distributing the elements in extended communion represents a kind of meal (as in a soup-kitchen or a canteen), this surely lacks the sense of corporateness that we usually associate with meals, and frankly obscures many of the typical meal-characteristics we have pointed up. In an article for *Worship*, P Rouillard, praised the renewed focus upon the eucharist as a meal, saying, 'Throughout the centuries the character of meal, and of communion meal, was gradually obscured . . . As a result of a great theological and liturgical effort during the last twenty years the Lord's Supper can once more be understood

---

77 'Shattered Liturgical Space: Questions Related to the Televising of Sunday Mass in French Canada' in *Studia Liturgica*, vol.24, no.1, (1994), pp 109-121
78 *Ibid.*, pp 109, 110, 114-5
79 *Ibid.*, pp 116, 117
80 *Ibid.*, p 117
81 'Preserving Unity at Large celebrations of the Eucharist' in D Holeton (ed), *Revising the Eucharist* (Alcuin/GROW Joint Liturgical Study, No.27, 1994) p 38

and experienced as a fraternal sacred meal'.[82] Surely extended communion frustrates this renewal and must be rejected as a retrograde step?

Nathan Mitchell: A Roman Catholic systematic perspective on extended communion

Our discussion about the shape of the liturgy, both in terms of a sequence of symbolic actions and as a fellowship meal, has revealed that by destroying the normative shape of the liturgy the eucharist loses some of its integrity. Separating communion from the rest of the celebration seems to place all the sacramental emphasis on receiving the elements at the expense of participating in the action as a whole. To truncate the liturgy in any other aspect would be considered unthinkable, so why can communion be separated off?

In his book, *Cult and Controversy*, Nathan Mitchell traces the history of extra-liturgical use of the eucharistic elements. While he accepts that the normative liturgical procedure is for communion to take place in the context of the full celebration, he allows that it can be postponed. Although Mitchell's chief interest is the cult of the mass—that is, the worship of the Host—much of what he proposes bears upon our discussion. In relation to our question, 'Why can communion be separated off?', Mitchell advances a view of the eucharist, on the basis of its character as action, which allows for the disruption.

Before considering Mitchell's argument, we must note that he writes from a Roman Catholic perspective. This has various consequences; the most important of which is that he is committed to uphold the doctrine of transubstantiation. Transubstantiation affirms an objective and persisting presence of Christ specifically located in the sacramental species. This understanding of real presence, and the kind of *ex opere operato* view of the eucharist with which it is associated, is not acceptable to many Anglicans. However, Mitchell's treatment of the extra-liturgical use of the elements is more comprehensive than that of any Anglican source, and, as we shall see, does not depend upon transubstantiation as its chief rationale. Moreover, in comparison with the Anglican Church, the question of extended communion and the cult of the eucharist has been debated more widely and for longer among Roman Catholics, it being a significantly commoner part of their spirituality. In the absence of a comparable Anglican alternative, therefore, it seems best to engage with Mitchell's esteemed and contemporary Roman Catholic perspective.

Mitchell recognizes that the tradition of receiving the elements outside the eucharist is ancient, but that so too is opposition to it. Therefore he asks whether communion outside mass is just a benign abnormality, historically ancient, but theologically disreputable.[83] Although he accepts that extended communion is 'a departure from the norm that is legitimate only when serious pastoral

---

82 'From Human Meal to Christian Eucharist' in *Worship* (quoted in R K Seasoltz, *Living Bread, Saving Cup*, (The Liturgical Press, Collegeville, Minn, 1982, 1987) p 146)

83 N Mitchell, *Cult and Controversy: The Worship of the Eucharist Outside Mass* (The Liturgical Press, Collegeville, Minnestota, 1990) p 253

circumstances require it', he nonetheless does not see it as entirely theologically reprehensible.[84] Included among the pastoral situations which Mitchell thinks might require extended communion, is a lack of priests. He argues that,

> 'In light of such pastoral situations, the theological significance [of extended communion] . . . becomes clearer. These liturgies of the presanctified intend to unite people not only with the Lord present in the eucharistic species, but also with the larger community and its liturgical action. To put it somewhat crudely, these rites are not primarily intended to make the Lord available, but to put people in touch with the action of the full eucharistic assembly . . . The sacramental symbols of bread and wine are not merely objects or relics that signify Jesus' presence; they are vital signs that signify and effect one's communion with the worshipping people of God. The . . . rites . . . thus invite us to a threefold communion: with the Lord, with the assembly, and with the full eucharistic action.' [85]

How does he imagine this connection is achieved? Mitchell suggests that an understanding of the true nature and dynamic of a sacrament provides the justification for extended communion. The crux lies in our understanding of symbols: 'symbols, even when lifted from their original matrix, continue to evoke that matrix and to make its power present among those who interact with the symbols. That is precisely why symbols can survive, even when their original context has been lost or altered'.[86]

> 'When the eucharist is distributed outside Mass, the original symbol matrix—the liturgical assembly of Christians gathered to give thanks, eat and drink—is eclipsed, but not destroyed . . . the sacramental symbols of eucharist continue to affirm the Lord's presence and the assembly's liturgical action, even though the celebration of Mass is over . . .; in the rites for communion outside Mass, the eucharistic elements retain their symbolic power to invite people into communion with the Lord and with one another. In other words, it is precisely because the eucharist is a sacramental symbol that its effectiveness survives even when its original matrix is eclipsed . . .'
> 'The theological justification for communion outside Mass must be rooted, therefore, in an understanding of sacramental symbols: what they are and how they work. Even when holy communion is separated from Mass, the sacramental elements retain their power as symbols, i.e., as invitations to the action of eating and drinking. Precisely because they are sacrament (and thus action, verb), the eucharistic food and drink may legitimately be reserved for the use of those who are prevented from participating in the liturgical assembly. The Christian custom of communicating persons outside Mass thus affirms rather than compromises or denies the sacramental nature of eucharistic liturgy.' [87]

84 *Ibid.*, p 254
85 *Ibid.*, p 255
86 *Ibid.*, p 256
87 *Ibid.*, p 258

Mitchell sees the liturgy follow the pattern action-object-action. The initial action of communal thanksgiving effects the consecration of the elements, which gives them a kind of objective status. However, this objectivity is at the same time a call to action, or at least to complete the action in communion. There is a verbal aspect inherent in the consecrated objects. According to this understanding, postponing the eucharistic action during its 'object-phase' is simply an extension of that action: the elements function like an aorist verb, which describes an action that has taken place, but has not necessarily ended. The character of the elements as sacramental—therefore verbal—objects ensures that 'the symbolic intentionality of the pattern . . . remains constant even when there is a delay between the two phases of community action—between the deed of liturgical praise and thanksgiving and the deed of eating and drinking'.[88]

Although Mitchell's explanation seems plausible, certain inherent weaknesses lead us to doubt whether it is satisfactory. The first thing to notice is that Mitchell introduces his theory in the context of a pastoral crisis: he says, 'In light of such pastoral situations, the theological significance [of extended communion] . . . becomes clearer. These liturgies of the presanctified intend to unite people not only with the Lord present in the eucharistic species, but also with the larger community and its liturgical action'. Our initial criticism must be that it is risky to build a theological principle on the basis of a pastoral crisis. As we have seen, extended communion is but one possible resolution to the problem of a dearth of priests. Thus to describe the sacrament in terms generated by an *ad hoc* solution seems precarious. No doubt the intention of extended communion is to link those receiving the elements that have been reserved *in via* with the eucharistic action as a whole, but that intention is not sufficient to legitimate the practice.

Our second criticism is of Mitchell's assertion that, 'these rites are not primarily intended to make the Lord available, but to put people in touch with the action of the full eucharistic assembly'. While we might take issue with his suggestion that 'making the Lord available' is not the primary purpose of extended communion, it is his second clause that concerns us. What is the full eucharistic assembly? Of course, in one sense, the eucharistic assembly is the catholic Church, the body of Christ scattered throughout the world and united with the company of heaven. It can also be described as that body of Christians that celebrates its faith in communion with its bishop—a venerable definition, dating back to St.Ignatius of Antioch in the first decade of the second century. However, much effort has been expended over the last century in trying to affirm the integrity of the local gathering of God's people, the local church, as the true and complete manifestation of the Church in a given place. The eucharistic community is therefore the body of Christ assembled locally for praise and fellowship. According to this definition, Mitchell's position becomes confused. It would seem that if the eucharistic community gathers it ought to celebrate the eucharist. Inevitably, Mitchell's Roman Catholic background will not countenance a

88 *Ibid.*, p 347

celebration without a priest, just as the Anglican Church will not. Two issues arise from this. The first concerns the relation of the congregation to the priest. Who is the celebrant of the eucharist, the priest or the whole Church? The Liturgical Movement has decided this question in favour of a corporate celebration, the priest operating simply as president. The eucharistic prayer begins with a dialogue (the *sursum corda*): 'It is clear that it functions not only as an invitation to the congregation to join in prayer, but also as the congregation's assent to the president's request to pray in their name'.[89] The second issue simply returns us to our original problem: 'Is extended communion the appropriate response to the pastoral problem?' Surely, if the eucharistic community, the *ekklesia*, has gathered, a eucharist should take place. It is hard to see how extended communion is a valid option, whatever its hypothetical merits as a link between congregations. The command to 'Do this' must take precedence.

A further related point concerns the original use of extended communion. The early Church extended communion when members of a congregation were absent for some reason. But it is important to notice that communion was extended from a specific congregation to a particular member of that congregation who was unable to take up his or her usual place at the weekly celebration. The same circumstances surround the contemporary practice of sick communion. The action takes place within one congregation of the body of Christ, one eucharistic community. Extended communion, as envisaged by Synod, involves at least two congregations, two separate eucharistic communities. Without any historical precedent, and without ecclesiological justification, the integrity of the local church is undermined. Although on some past occasions one church has passed over a portion of its elements to another as a sign of unity (e.g. the ancient *fermentum* or the *Sancta*[90]), in each case, the receiving community has not been deprived of its own eucharist.

Our final major criticism of Mitchell relates to his understanding of the symbolic world, or 'matrix'. His description is pertinent; but it is also problematic. He seems to imply that the significance of the elements is relative to the ritual context. While this is certainly true in part, the 'strong' doctrine of consecration held by Roman Catholics cannot grant that it is the symbolic matrix alone that gives bread and wine their significance. In discussion of the sacraments, theories about symbols cannot be divorced from questions of ontology. The effects of liturgical consecration must be *objective*, not simply *relative*. For a Roman Catholic, it is this, rather than any symbolic explanation, that substantiates the cult of the mass. This cannot, of course, be said of Anglicans. To insist upon such a doctrine as a defence of extended communion would be entirely unacceptable to many in the Church of England.

Leaving questions of real presence aside for the time being, a further aspect of this criticism must be considered. We have argued before now that the

---

89   D J Kennedy & D Mann, *Making the Eucharistic Prayer Work* (Grove Worship Series, No.103, 1998), p 17
90   N Mitchell, *op.cit.*, pp 35;57-8.

'meaning' of the eucharist cannot be identified with the elements alone. The eucharist comprises various symbolic actions in its symbolic matrix. So, even if we grant Mitchell his description of the eucharist's symbolic world, we cannot allow that one part of this world, extended from it, can encapsulate the whole. We are back to our former discussion about the shape of the liturgy. To share in the eucharist, whether or not it is described as a symbolic matrix, requires more than just the reception of its object, or symbolic 'product'.

A few further observations should be made before we move on. The first is that Mitchell's basic subject is different from ours. He is describing the history of the eucharistic cult and developing a modern justification for it; whereas we are attempting to discover how extended communion will affect the sacramental piety of the Church of England. This is most significant where Mitchell assumes that the cult is part of the full and regular round of eucharistic devotion in any place, involving a regular celebration of the eucharist. In such a context it is possible to see how adoration of the Host derives from and leads back to the full eucharistic action. The 'verbal' character of the 'object-phase' is easily assimilated. If, however, the community is deprived of the eucharist, this will not necessarily be intelligible.

Returning briefly to the matter of symbols, we should note that symbols are a human operation, not an object. This means that symbols can mean different things to different people in different times or circumstances.[91] The very history of the cult itself bears witness to this. As the laity became increasingly cut off from communion during the Middle Ages, their eucharistic devotion changed from communication to observation. In order to safeguard the sacramental imagination, then, it would seem to be essential to preserve the integrity of the eucharistic action. Furthermore, the eucharistic *anamnesis* is not simply a verbal remembering, a recalling of 'what we (or someone else) did before in the eucharistic action'. The command to 'Do this in remembrance of me' applies to the action in its entirety, celebrated by each congregation. Mitchell's theory is helpful insofar as it aims to link the receivers with the full action, but that is not ultimately what eucharist is about. It is about our thanksgiving offered to God, who, through the work of his Son, calls together and creates each local *ekklesia*. In addition, we might well ask whether, in a truly united liturgical action, the verbal call to communion comes from the Liturgy of the Word, rather than from some symbolic verbal characteristic of the elements?

What has emerged from our discussion so far is that extended communion breaks up the liturgical action in a way that is hard to justify. This first part of our investigation was a response to the view that eucharistic piety revolves around reception of the elements. It should be clear by now that eucharistic piety, if it is to do justice to the liturgical integrity of the sacrament, cannot be allowed to rest solely upon communion.

---

91 J Gelineau, *The Liturgy: Today and Tomorrow* (DLT, London, 1978) p 96

3
Extended Communion and Real Presence

The second observation we made about the decision to authorize *Public Worship with Communion by Extension* was that it might precipitate the Church of England into a debate about the independence of the consecrated elements. One aspect of Mitchell's theory that we did not discuss was his statement that, 'These liturgies of the presanctified intend to unite people . . . with the Lord present in the eucharistic species'. For a Roman Catholic, committed to the doctrine of transubstantiation, this statement is straightforward. Anglicans, however, are not clearly committed to any doctrine of real presence. In fact, it would doubtless be possible to find Anglicans who subscribe to any one of the numerous definitions of real presence (and probably some undefined ones as well). Many people in the Church of England have only a vague comprehension of the questions concerning consecration and presence. Extended communion, in which the only tangible link with the eucharist is the elements, is confusing without a clear doctrine of Christ's presence mediated through communion. Other members of the Church have much more strident views about these questions, and may be either repelled or elated by the prospect of extended communion. So, despite Synod's deliberate attempt to avoid any questions about reservation—the traditional battlefield for questions of real presence[92]—the issue almost certainly cannot be avoided; and Synod may (perhaps unwittingly) already have taken sides.

Synod and Consecration
The heart of our question about extended communion is, 'Can we have a united eucharistic action divided between different congregations?' which, if answered affirmatively, entails the question, 'What provides the link between the full celebration and the receiving congregation?' Now, we have already raised serious doubts about splitting up the eucharistic action, but we must investigate Synod's answer to this second question.

The debate about extended communion provoked a number of responses concerning the status of the elements: 'The conveying of the elements for the purpose of Extended Communion is considered by some to be both meaningless and unscriptural'.[93] Although the reason for this sentiment is not stated explicitly, it seems reasonable to assume that questions about consecration lie behind it. Synod, however, dodges the issue in its response:

> '[T]he administration of Holy Communion involves in every case a conveying or carrying of the elements from the Lord's Table to the communicants. Extended Communion involves an extension of the movement of the elements, over which the full Prayer of Thanksgiving has been recited, from the Lord's

---

92   Cf. GS1230Y, §11.c.
93   GSMisc 452, §3.b.

Table in church to the worshippers . . . in another church. The type of provision which the House proposes . . . will ensure that there is no undue extension in time, and the extension of distance will be limited by the cure or group of team parishes for which permission is given. Thus congregations for which Extended Communion may be authorised will already be held together by bonds of fellowship and may be considered, for this purpose, to be a single worshipping community locally divided. We consider this understanding of Extended Communion to be entirely consonant with scripture, and we are clear that provision of this sort is not inconsistent with Article xxv, which in its reference to *"carrying about"* the sacraments was aimed at a quite different practice. In any case, the issue whether one understanding of *"consecration"* or another is implied by the movement of the elements does not arise. The Lord is present everywhere; what is moved or carried within an extended worshipping community are the material elements which are the appointed means of participation in the reality of his body and blood.'[94]

The substance of this defence seems confused. Clearly Synod wishes to avoid a debate about consecration; but the explanation given for this, and various other comments, automatically raise important questions about real presence. First, Synod goes out of its way to assert that 'the full Prayer of Thanksgiving has been recited' over the elements, which cannot but be a reference to consecration; then it provides a somewhat vague description of the relation of Christ's presence to the elements ('The Lord is present everywhere . . .'). It is hard to believe that many (especially anglo-catholic) Anglicans would be satisfied with this generalized explanation. Furthermore, the statement about time-limits is probably a device introduced to avoid questions about reservation. We judge, therefore, that, despite Synod's statement to the contrary, the issue of consecration does arise.

The reference to Article xxv is important. In words echoing Article xxv, Article xxviii states that 'The Sacrament of the Lord's Supper was not by Christ's ordinance reserved, carried about, lifted up, or worshipped'. These two Articles lay behind much of the dispute over reservation both before and after the failure of the 1928 revision of the Prayer Book. Only recently has the Church permitted the elements to be 'carried about' for the purpose of sick communion, and not without dissent. This wariness is partly due to a concern to avoid any supposedly idolatrous use of the sacrament (such as Benediction); but it is also the response of a sacramental theology that questions the significance of the eucharistic species outside the context of the celebration—a view that has some affinity with the theology of the Reformers, which lay behind Cranmer's decision to ban extended communion. If these two Articles refer to questions of consecration, then Synod's claim that Article xxv does not relate to the question at hand is only true in part.

An Ecclesiological Connection?
Another area of confusion surrounds Synod's explanation of the relationship between congregations. It attempts to show that conveying the elements from the altar to

94 GSMisc 452, §3.b

people outside the confines of the celebrating church is different only in terms of distance from their distribution to those within. The reason given for this is that the geographically divided recipients are part of a larger worshipping community. We have already discussed the issue of the integrity of each local eucharistic community, and maintain that where the eucharistic community gathers there ought to be a eucharist. We might also point out that, according to Synod's logic, a better solution to the pastoral problem would be to encourage congregations to merge, since they are, after all, one worshipping community (sic). It would be much better for the congregation to go to the elements—and so join in the full celebration—than for the elements to go to the congregation. Of course, one could argue that people cannot be expected to travel a long way to church; but in some places Roman Catholics in England have for many years had to travel miles to attend mass. Although this arrangement is not entirely satisfactory, it is certainly preferable to extended communion. However, a more likely impediment to such a scheme would probably be resistance on behalf of the congregations themselves to any idea that they are 'a single worshipping community' (as anyone will know who has been involved in parochial reorganization). Synod's assumptions are thus undermined.

Besides these slightly light-hearted criticisms, there is a more serious one; for according to Synod's logic, each congregation is part of a much larger unit in the cure of the diocesan, and ultimately provincial, bishop.[95] As we already know, this description of the eucharistic community is ancient. So we could ask, 'Given that historically and doctrinally the bishop is the chief minister of the eucharist, would it not make more sense for the bishop to celebrate one eucharist, the elements from which could then be distributed among the priestless parishes in his cure?' Such an arrangement would certainly be a powerful symbol of unity, and is entirely consonant with Synod's description of ecclesiological relationships. The problem with such a plan is that ever since the emergence of the presbyteral eucharist, discrete congregations have enjoyed their own presbyteral eucharist under the sacramental aegis of the bishop. The development of presbyteral eucharists was itself a response to a pastoral situation in which the bishop was unable to preside at a single congregation of the body of Christ. Presumably, in endorsing this change, the early Church was rejecting any idea that extending communion from the episcopal eucharist to the parishes was an adequate form of eucharistic piety. So it would seem that Synod's assumptions, though based upon a valid ecclesiology, do not legitimate the practice of extended communion among local groups of churches.

The Elements as the Link
Even if we do not reject Synod's explanation of the relation between parishes, we are still left with the question, 'In extended communion, what links the receiving congregation to the full celebration of the eucharist by another congregation?' Commenting on a draft rite for *Sunday Worship with Holy Communion in the Absence of a Priest*, Synod remarked, 'There is now a much

95   *Ibid.,* §3.c

clearer statement in the rite of the relationship between this act of worship and that from which the consecrated elements are brought'. Turning to the recently authorized liturgy itself we see this in two statements that the minister is directed to make. First, at the Gathering:

'In union with those who celebrate (have celebrated) the Eucharist at *N* . . . this day, we seek God's grace in Holy Communion. For as often as we eat this bread and drink this cup in obedience to his command, we proclaim the Lord's death until he comes.'[96]

Then after the Peace:

'In fellowship with the whole Church of God, with all who have been brought together by the Holy Spirit to worship on this day, and particularly with our brothers and sisters at *N* . . . who have celebrated the Eucharist, let us rejoice that we are called to be part of the body of Christ.'[97]

The second of these is clearly intended to emphasize the unity of the local church with the whole body of Christ. We have already made some observations about this aspect of extended communion. The first quotation contains other inferences. Chief among these is the implication that it is the *communion* that provides the link between the receiving parish and the eucharist, and that fulfils the Lord's command. In other words, it is the elements that are the focus in the sacramental exchange. According to the Synod documents, the only clear link between the receiving congregation and the eucharist is the elements; thus there is an implicit suggestion that the full benefit of the eucharist derives from reception of the consecrated elements. Many members of the Church of England would flatly disagree, and concur with Buchanan's judgement that 'a naked distribution is highly defective at all sorts of levels'.[98]

Buchanan's comment comes from a paragraph in which he discusses 'the role of the eucharistic prayer'.[99] This is the crux of the issue. It is not hard to imagine that Christians who treat the Lord's Supper as a plain memorial of Christ, a fellowship meal conducted in obedience to his command to 'Do this', would see no point in receiving bread and wine outside the context of the full Supper-action. Without any idea of presence, the action is meaningless: it fails to obey the command, and the bread and wine are just normal bread and wine. Only with a 'stronger' view of consecration does the action begin to make sense; but Synod refuses to debate this point.

Consecration and the Rite for Extended Communion

A further complication arises concerning consecration, for the contemporary Anglican position on this subject, as articulated by the Liturgical Commission, refuses to admit of a 'moment' or 'formula' of consecration; rather, consecration is the product of the Thanksgiving (*eucharistia*) as a whole. For example, in its

---

96 *Public Worship with Communion by Extension*
97 *Ibid.*
98 D Smethurst, *op.cit.*, p 21
99 *Ibid.*, p 21

commentary on Holy Communion Series 3, the Liturgical Commission says:

'If the thirteenth or the seventeenth centuries saw fit to have "moments" of consecration at the recitation of the dominical words within the narrative of institution, we cannot now be bound by these precedents. History suggests that emphasis upon such "moments" not only gives the rite a false climax at this point, but also distracts from the understanding of the prayer as being above all a *thanksgiving*; and if we lose that understanding we are failing in part to carry out our Lord's command to the best of our ability.' [100]

James Dallen makes a similar point, which ties in with what we have already said about the integrity of the liturgical action:

'Characteristic of recent liturgical theology is the recognition of the unity of the eucharistic prayer. Less and less, even in popular understanding, is it regarded as merely the setting for the institution narrative. The "words of consecration" are likewise given less emphasis, with the whole prayer from start to finish seen as consecratory.' [101]

This explanation presents us with two problems. On the one hand, those who refuse to accept ideas of objective presence will feel that the 'meaning' of the eucharistic elements derives from their context in the fellowship meal. For if communion is receiving the body of Christ, and if this is inherently linked with thanksgiving, to divorce the two might be construed as to empty communion of its significance. On the other hand, if the proposed rite for extended communion included any form of thanksgiving, the question arises, 'When is thanksgiving eucharistic, and so consecratory, and when is it not?' Judging by the Synod reports, this question received much attention. Commenting on a draft rite, Synod says that no thanksgivings were introduced that might 'import a "feel" in the rite too closely akin to the form of the eucharistic prayer'.[102] However, there is a prayer that reads as follows:

> Blessed are you,
> God of those who hunger and thirst:
> for you give us our food in due season.
> You nourish us with your word
> which is the bread of life.
> You strengthen us with your Spirit,
> the new wine of your kingdom.
> In Christ you are food for the hungry,
> refreshment for the weary.
> Blessed are you our Creator and Redeemer.
> Blessed be God forever. [103]

Now according to traditional sources, the eucharistic thanksgiving incorporates various themes, such as praise for creation and redemption, etc. This prayer, though carefully avoiding any specific mention of the elements, or

100 Liturgical Commission, *A Commentary on Holy Communion Series 3* (SPCK, London, 1971) p 23
101 'The Congregation's Share in the Eucharistic Prayer' in *Worship*. Seasoltz, *op. cit.*, p 113
102 GS1230Y, §27
103 *Public Worship with Communion by Extension*

of the institution narrative, certainly has resonances of a eucharistic kind, and this is surely deliberate. Furthermore, a rubric is included shortly before the Peace that says, 'Thanksgiving and praise may be offered for the great acts of God in creation and redemption'.[104] There is a danger of blurring the boundary between eucharistic prayer and non-eucharistic thanksgiving. The issue becomes all the more serious when we consider that much ink has been spilt over the inclusion of the traditional Roman thanksgiving at the Preparation of the Gifts in the full eucharistic rite ('Blessed are you, Lord, God of all creation. Through your goodness we have this bread/wine to offer/set before you. . . .'). For some, this additional thanksgiving over the gifts encroaches upon the specific thanksgiving of the eucharistic prayer.[105]

The fact that Synod rightly refuses to allow that a consecration takes place in the rite for extended communion points us to the central issue. The key distinction concerns the use of the Institution Narrative, even though contemporary Anglican theology eschews any formulaic approach to consecration. It is interesting at this point to note the debate concerning the Institution Narrative conducted by Synod.

'The most consistent and frequently expressed concern on the part of those making submissions to the Committee was that the proposed form of service would be unacceptable if it did not include some explicit reference to the institution of the Eucharist at the Last Supper. It was equally clear from the submissions that any use of the narrative of Institution which suggested that it was being used in a "consecratory" way would be equally unacceptable to another range of those making submissions. The Committee has concluded that a reference to the Institution should be included as an invariable element in the minister's spoken introduction. In this position it is intended to "place" a service which includes the distribution of consecrated elements in a clear and explicit relation to the Eucharist and its institution at the Lord's Supper, but at a point in the rite where it could not be mistakenly thought of as being a eucharistic prayer. The choice of the narrative from the gospel of Luke has been a deliberate use of a form of the Institution Narrative which is clearly drawn from the gospels but is not cast in the form usually associated with the Narrative in the eucharistic prayer.'[106]

Churches of the Reformed tradition use the Institution Narrative as a warrant text. However, the Church of England, like the Roman Catholic Church, places the dominical words within the eucharistic prayer itself. The implication is that the prayer is intended to be *performative*: the 'is' of 'This is my body/blood' becomes the prayer of the Church over the elements in the expectation that the Lord's words will be fulfilled. Synod's decision to put the Institution Narrative 'at a point in the rite where it could not be mistakenly thought of as being a eucharistic prayer' seems to betray the current Anglican insistence that it does not have a formulaic approach to

104 *Ibid.*
105 Cf. Colin Buchanan, *The End of the Offertory* (Grove Liturgical Study, No. 14, 1978) pp 39-40
106 GS1230Y, §24

consecration. What Synod says, in effect, is that the controversy over whether the rite for extended communion should include the words of Institution, is basically a controversy over the question of consecration. The reference to people making 'submissions' from different 'ranges' (presumably meaning 'church-parties') reveals the doctrinal diversity present in the Church of England, and suggests that the question of extended communion cannot escape the debate over presence. If we are right in judging that, for extended communion to be meaningful or efficacious, it requires a 'strong' doctrine of consecration, Synod may unintentionally be assuming a 'higher' view than would please some members of the Church.

Extended Communion and Real Presences

Despite this latest observation, there are pointers in a different direction. For example, the original report by the House of Bishops laid down certain theological principles which must govern any discussion of extended communion. Among these were the insistence that 'the Christ who is present in the sacramental mode is the same Christ who is present wherever two or three are gathered together in Christ's name', and the explanation that 'wherever we hear the Word we feed on the same living Christ as we receive under the form of bread and wine'.[107] Although it is not made explicit, these relate to an increasingly common perspective on the eucharist involving the idea of 'real presences'.

In a discussion of the variety of emphases given to word and sacrament in different Christian traditions, John Macquarrie asserts the complementary nature of their relationship: 'In the word and sacraments, the divine presence is focused so as to communicate itself to us with a directness and intensity like that of the incarnation itself, which indeed is re-presented in the proclaiming of the word and in the celebration of the sacraments'.[108] Macquarrie defends the view that Christ is made present in different aspects of the liturgy. To illustrate this, he points to the traditional ceremonial of the eucharist: 'At the reading of the gospel, the book is elevated, for at that moment it has become the focus of the divine presence and action; whereas after the consecration, the host is elevated as the focus of Christ's presence'.[109] Now while Macquarrie is clear that the verbal and sacramental modes of Christ's presence are not the same, he nonetheless asserts that 'the very difference between word and sacraments makes each of them necessary to each other': neither may be given priority.[110]

Mitchell also introduces a view of 'the many modes of Christ's presence'.[111] Like Macquarrie he recognizes the importance of both word and sacrament in mediating Christ's presence. He uses Cyril of Jerusalem's view of the 'Two Tables— Word and Sacrament' to illustrate his point, saying, 'The two tables are regarded . . . as a single source of nourishment'.[112] Furthermore, he explains that Christ's presence in the sacrament cannot be made sense of 'without having first noted the

107 GS1082, §8
108 J Macquarrie, *Principles of Christian Theology* (SCM, London, revised edition 1977) p 449
109 *Ibid.*, pp 449-450
110 *Ibid.*, pp 450-451
111 N Mitchell, *op.cit.*, p 243
112 *Ibid.*, pp 245-246, 247

presence of Christ in the assembly itself, in the Word, and in the liturgical ministers who serve'.[113] He goes on to say that 'Christ's real presence originates in the liturgical praxis of the assembly'.[114] Christ's distinctive presence in the bread and wine is part of a larger symbolic pattern: 'The Lord's presence touches this pattern at all points—not merely at the moment of consecration in the eucharist.'[115]

The concept of real presences has only emerged lately owing to new perspectives on the eucharist. At some time in its history, the Church lost the vision of the Christian assembly as the body of Christ. In an article entitled 'Transubstantiation, Transfinalization, Transignification', Edward Schillebeeckx discusses this change in understanding. He argues that,

'Holy scripture, the writings of the patristic age, and medieval scholasticism, in contrast to the theology of the post-Tridentine era, always emphasised the *res sacramenti*. Obviously, this presence of Christ in our hearts (*res sacramenti*) is brought about through the medium of the sacred host, and this implies the real presence of Christ in the host. Yet, the emphasis is placed not on the eucharistic presence but upon the *purpose* of this presence, the presence of Christ *in us*. It is for this purpose ultimately that the sacrament of the eucharist was instituted by Christ ... Forced by circumstances and already preceded in this by medieval piety, post-Tridentine theology shifted the emphasis. The *res sacramenti* was pushed into the background, while the *res et sacramentum*, that is, the real presence in the sacred host, was emphasised so much that it seemed to be an end in itself and not a *res et sacramentum*, that is, totally oriented toward the *res ultima*: the growth of Christ in the heart of the community.' [116]

Schillebeeckx recommends that we 'replace the emphasis where the New Testament, the fathers, and the great scholastic theologians placed it, that is, on the *res sacramenti*, the end for which Christ instituted it'.[117] In this change of emphasis, real presence becomes a more generic term. This is not to deny the real presence of Christ in the eucharistic elements—and Schillebeeckx happily defends the eucharistic cult;[118] but it does mean that our understanding of engagement with Christ present in the eucharist has to be multi-faceted: it cannot be related solely to a local presence in relation to the elements. This recognition undermines any notion that a eucharistic piety can be reduced to communion alone.

Extended Communion and Epiklesis

A final issue concerning questions about consecration and presence arises out of G Austin's comment that 'eucharistic reality is about a conversion: not only of the elements of bread and wine but of the gathered assembly of the baptised'.[119]

113 *Ibid.*, p 243
114 *Ibid.*, p 244
115 *Ibid.*, p 349
116 'Transubstantiation, Transfinalization, Transignification' in *Worship*. Seasoltz, *op.cit.* pp 186-7
117 *Ibid.*, p 187
118 *Ibid.*, p 187
119 G Austin, 'Communion Service: A Break With Tradition?' in G Austin (ed), *Fountain of Life* (Pastoral Press, Washington DC, 1991) p 128.

The *epiklesis*, so Austin argues, applies as much to the *ekklesia* as to the elements. Here we can see in operation a eucharistic ecclesiology reminiscent of McPartlan's work. McPartlan himself says, 'Modern liturgical studies have taught us to widen our gaze from the elements of bread and wine on the Lord's table, to heed the assembly which is gathered round and to understand the Eucharist as the entire celebration of God's people within which the elements are transformed'.[120] The crucial issue is not what is *on* the table, but who is *at* the table.[121] Both the eucharist and the Church can be called the body of Christ. Likewise, Mitchell affirms that,

'[T]he church's celebration of a ritual meal launches a process of becoming eucharist, a process that is completed only when Christians recognise their own identity as Christ's body in the world. That is why the epiklesis of the eucharistic prayer prays not only for a transformation of the gifts but also of the people . . . Or as Augustine expressed it in Book VII of his Confessions: "I am the food of grown men and women. Grow, and you shall feed on me. You will not change me into yourself, as you change food into your flesh, but you will be changed into me".'[122]

This conception of eucharistic ecclesiology leads us back to the theology of the parish communion. Part of the original impetus for reform derived from the observation by men like Hebert that the eucharist is the great meeting-point of God's people at which they truly become the Church and are transformed for witness in the world. Christopher Irvine tells us that 'one of Gabriel's favourite Patristic texts was a phrase from a sermon of Augustine of Hippo, in which he tells his hearers that they are to become what they receive, the Body of Christ'.[123] It is only as the body of Christ that Christians can offer the world a model of what human society ought to be—an idea reflecting the influence of the great Christian social thinker, F D Maurice. But there is more than this: in the eucharist, society is transformed, 'for all that the Christian brings to the eucharistic assembly, as an individual and a member of the wider community, "is reoriented towards God as its centre, and is transformed, sanctified and glorified"'.[124] Hebert's theology rested on the assumption that the Church becomes the mystical body of Christ in the eucharist—in theological terms, he expounds a eucharistic ecclesiology. The *epiklesis* is more than the calling down of the Holy Spirit upon the gifts of bread and wine: it is a prayer for the transformation of the eucharistic community as it gathers to celebrate the sacrament of the body of Christ. It is worth noting in this respect that the new *Common Worship* eucharistic prayers give a prominent place to the invocation of the Spirit over both gifts and congregation.[125]

120 P McPartlan, *Sacrament of Salvation* (T&T Clark, Edinburgh, 1997) p xiv
121 Cf. N Mitchell's account of L E Klosinski's doctoral thesis, 'The Meals in Mark', in *Real Presence: The Work of the Eucharist* (Liturgical Training Publications, Chicago,1998) pp 69, 77
122 *Ibid.*, pp 118-9
123 C Irvine, *Worship, Church, and Society* (Canterbury Press, 1993) p 113
124 *Ibid.*, p 113.
125 This is most evident in Order One Prayers F, G and H, which follow the eastern pattern of a concluding 'united' epiklesis over elements and people (as opposed to the 'split epiklesis' common to the western tradition).

4
Some Further Issues

Eucharist and Unity

Before concluding our study, we must consider a number of further issues. The first concerns the relationship between eucharist and unity. The Parish Communion grew up first among anglo-catholics. However, its proponents were adamant that it should not become identified with any Church party.[126] Though anglo-catholic themselves, Hebert and his colleagues occupied much more of a middle ground, and hoped to draw people into a broad consensus. In his 'Translator's Preface' to Yngwe Brilioth's *Eucharistic Faith and Practice*, Hebert wrote:

> 'Those who kneel together at the same altar are often conscious of serious differences and of mutual suspicion; yet the fact that they kneel together at the altar is the symbol and the instrument of a unity deeper than their differences.'[127]

Extended communion endangers this vision of the Church. If, as we suspect, extended communion will recommend itself largely only to those who hold a strong view of real presence, it may well become the preserve of anglo-catholics, while evangelicals might simply abandon eucharistic centrality. In the latter case, there is, in fact, already some evidence that this is happening. From the beginning, evangelicals were suspicious of the Parish Communion. Buchanan gives several reasons for this.[128] It was seen by some as off-putting to newcomers: people on the fringe of the Church can find their way more easily into non-sacramental worship, for sacramental worship inevitably excludes them. Also, the parish communion often saw a reduction in preaching. In order to stay within reasonable time-limits, the service had to be pruned somewhere, and the sermon was the obvious candidate. Another problem, derived from the slogan 'The Lord's service for the Lord's people on the Lord's day', was that the parish communion became so much the centre of Sunday worship that Sunday evening congregations dwindled. In many evangelical parishes, Sunday evenings were a focus for young people, and after-church activities had a place almost as important as church ones. If evening church ceased or became thin, a loss of committed young people seemed likely to follow. Finally, the idea that the eucharist is the panacea for all spiritual ills seemed intolerably anglo-catholic. By contrast, Buchanan describes the prevalent evangelical view which saw the eucharist 'as a kind of spiritual treat, to be used sparingly—topping up the spiritual diet rather than being a basic ingredient of it'.[129] Coupled with this undercurrent of suspicion is the growing extent of experimentation with new forms of worship. The appearance

---

126 A G Hebert, *Liturgy and Society* (Faber & Faber, London, 1935) pp vii-viii
127 Y Brilioth, *Eucharistic Faith and Practice; Evangelical and Catholic* (SPCK, London, 1930; tr. A G Hebert, 1939) p ix
128 Colin Buchanan, *The Heart of Sunday Worship* (Grove Worship Series No. 121, 1992) p 12
129 *Ibid.*, p 12

of 'Family Services', and the attraction of charismatic worship—which emphasizes immediate rather than mediated (e.g. sacramental) religious experience—has already threatened the parish eucharist. Extended communion can hardly fail to hasten the move back to non-eucharistic worship in some places. Given the propensity of catholics to emphasise the sacraments, and the traditional evangelical affinity for the word, we may see the development of two different forms of piety. Added to this is the increased polarization of some evangelicals and some anglo-catholics, which is already threatening to divide the Church. Extended communion therefore appears as a betrayal of the principles that inspired the eucharistic focus it is intended to maintain.

Lex Orandi Lex Credendi

Closely related to this last point is the question of the didactic function of liturgy. At the beginning of *The Parish Communion*, Hebert announced that, 'There is a whole mentality to be transformed, if a new understanding of our life in the Church is to be gained'.[130] The chief aim of the book was not to make 'a plea for' parish communions, but to 'set forth a conception of the Church, which appears to compel the adoption of the Parish Communion as its necessary expression in liturgy.'[131] From an early date there were general fears about the parish communion being adopted without an appreciation of the underlying theology and appropriate teaching to accompany it. One of Michael Ramsey's *Durham Essays* highlights this concern.[132] However, Ramsey goes on to say that the Holy Communion 'will be its own interpreter and teacher. For the supreme question is not what we make of the Eucharist but what the Eucharist is making of us, as (together with the Word) it fashions us into the way of Christ'.[133] What both Ramsey and Hebert recognized was the intimate relationship between liturgy and learning, enshrined in Anglicanism's first principle, *lex orandi lex credendi*. We must bring this insight to bear on the question of extended communion.

'Making my communion'

Despite the injection of social thought that the parish communion movement gave to the Anglican perspective on the eucharist, the problem of individualism persists in relation to communion. The idea that I go to church to 'make *my* communion' is unlikely to be subverted by a service in which the full eucharistic celebration of the people of God is reduced to an individual reception of the elements. Furthermore, the idea of a 'right' to communion is almost implicit in the provision of extended communion.[134] We must strongly resist such a view. Concerning the growth of general communion engendered by the parish eucharist, Ramsey said, 'The awe in the individual's approach to Holy

---

130 A G Hebert, *The Parish Communion*, p vii
131 *Ibid.*, p vii
132 'The Parish Communion' in *Durham Essays and Addresses*, p 20
133 *Ibid.*, p 21
134 Witness Synod's determination not to deprive people of the communion they have come to expect (as if by right?).

Communion which characterised both the Tractarians and the Evangelicals of old, stands in contrast to the ease with which our congregations come tripping to the altar week by week'.[135] How much more will this problem be exacerbated by extended communion? While it is, of course, right that Christians expect to celebrate holy communion, the provision of the rite should not become so indiscriminate in character as to detract from the rightful sense of reverence with which we approach God's seat of mercy. The sacrament is a gift from God, not a human right. As Philippe Barras says, outside its normal ritual context,

'receiving communion can lead to, or promote, an individualistic understanding of the eucharist and come to appear as a personal right. The absence of epiklesis and of consecration puts, ritually for the congregation, the eucharistic bread outside the reciprocal movement of a gift and counter-gift which is made real by the Spirit and which leads us to giving up our lives for our brothers and sisters.'[136]

This one example of the way liturgy can affect theology suffices to urge caution on those who oversee liturgical change, and especially any change that involves a drastic alteration in so central a service of worship as the eucharist.

The Integrity of the Local Church as the Celebrant of the Liturgy

A number of other concerns about the effect extended communion may have on sacramental imagination should be noted. There is an inherent danger that extended communion may undermine the efforts of liturgical scholars to inculcate a view of the eucharist that emphasizes the importance of each aspect of the rite. From a German Roman Catholic perspective, Helmut Büsse reckons that extended communion reflects 'a certain view of the eucharist which has grown over decades, often narrowly defined and misunderstood, that says that a Mass equals the reception of communion'.[137] There is clearly a danger that everything we have said about the liturgical errors implicit in extended communion may creep into the theological understanding of those who experience it. Not least among these is a view of the eucharist which sees it as an object to be received rather than an action in which to participate. In addition, other areas of confusion might ensue concerning the relation between the clergy and laity and about the integrity of the local church. It needs to be emphasised that the eucharist flows from the body of Christ, the *ekklesia*, not from ordination, and that each local eucharistic community is the full and complete presence of the Church in a given place. Extended communion is more likely to engender a view of the priest as celebrant rather than president of the liturgy, and it is hard to see how a sense of dependency (as opposed to integrity) can be excluded from the perspective of the receiving congregation.

---

135 *Ibid.*, p 19
136 'Symposium: Sunday Assemblies in the Absence of a Priest: The Situation and Trends in France' in *Studia Liturgica*, vol.26, no.1, (1996), pp 102-3
137 *Ibid.*, p 108

Practical Concerns

A final area of concern is the actual practice of *Public Worship with Communion by Extension*. Evidence for this is largely anecdotal, though the 'Notes' and 'Guidelines' included in the official rite suggest that there was already some anxiety about how extended communion might be used prior to its publication. Reports of 'offertory processions' of the extended elements, 'taking' and 'breaking' the pre-consecrated bread, gestures of thanksgiving in relation to the gifts, tabernacles and aumbries stuffed with a month's supply of consecrated hosts for use by Lay Readers at the 8 o'clock and other exaggerated interpretations of the limits of extension (in time and place), and various other abuses suggest that practitioners are not reading and abiding by the regulations and that training is not being adequately and uniformly applied.[138] Such errors can only increase the potential damage that may be done to our sacramental imagination and understanding.

---

138 For a practical introduction to the new liturgy, see P Tovey, *Public Worship with Communion by Extension: A Commentary* (Grove Worship Series No.167, Grove Books Ltd, Cambridge, 2001).

5
Conclusion

We began our study with a number of concerns, chief among which was the question whether extended communion achieves its basic goal of sustaining the current eucharistic piety of the Church of England. In conclusion we answer that it does not. This judgement is made on several bases. First, Synod fails to recognize that the centrality of eucharistic worship is not simply a piety revolving around communion. By examining the principles that have guided the Church's liturgical reforms in the last few decades, we discovered that extended communion transgresses many of them. Despite the defence of extended communion proposed by Nathan Mitchell, we concluded that separating communion from the eucharist damages the liturgical integrity of the rite.

Our second major field of investigation was a response to the weight extended communion places on the elements themselves. Although Synod claims that extended communion does not raise questions about consecration and presence, we found that encounter with these issues is unavoidable. Likewise, we discovered that Synod's attempt to provide an ecclesiological link between extending and receiving congregations fails to satisfy, and that the only discernible link is the elements themselves. This led us to investigate how a 'naked distribution' of the elements could support a eucharistic piety. It seemed likely that it could only be meaningful or efficacious if it was supported by a 'strong' view of consecration—a view that is not acceptable to many Anglicans. Furthermore, we noted that certain ideas expressed in the synodical papers introduced a further issue—real presences. The complementary nature of different modes of Christ's presence, not least between word and sacrament, is enshrined in the liturgy, and any liturgical revision must take account of this.

Finally, we considered a number of possible eventualities if extended communion becomes widespread and frequent. First, it may drive a wedge between Catholics and Evangelicals in the Church of England owing to its dependence on a 'high' doctrine of presence. A potential corollary of this might be that the original purpose of extended communion (to safeguard eucharistic centrality) is undermined as some congregations return to non-eucharistic forms of worship. Secondly, owing to the close relationship between liturgy, understanding and belief (*lex orandi lex credendi*), extended communion may hinder the assimilation of important aspects of eucharistic theology concerning its social dynamic, the role of the laity, and the integrity of the local church.

In conclusion, therefore, we suggest that extended communion is a poor solution to the Church of England's pastoral problem. Eucharistic piety cannot be identified with communion alone: the Christian eucharist is a profound mystery, and to truncate it in any aspect is mistaken. It is impossible to maintain that extended communion is anything but a 'second best' alternative, and the plain fact is that Sunday worship with communion by extension is Sunday worship without the eucharist. Hence, with so many concerns raised about extended communion, we judge that *Public Worship with Communion by Extension* must be regarded as a provisional and temporary measure. In the meantime, however, we still face our basic pastoral problem: the number of priests is insufficient to meet the proper sacramental expectations of the laity, bearing in mind that, as a matter of principle, this expectation demands a full eucharistic celebration.

In order to face up to this problem we need to reassess the situation. Lying behind our wide-ranging criticism of extended communion is the simple observation that, instead of repairing the deficit in eucharistic ministers, General Synod has decided to tamper with the eucharist itself. In other words, there is a basic mismatch involved in using extended communion as a liturgical solution to an ecclesiastical problem. So, rather than upset the Church's worship—the primary Christian activity—the obvious way forward is to think hard about the future of ministry. In this respect, it is interesting to note that ten years ago the American RC bishops published *Gathered Steadfast in the Faith* (subtitled 'Sunday Worship in the Absence of a Priest'), in which they observe that the root problem— the lack of priests—remains unresolved and warn that 'Sunday Worship in the Absence of a Priest' may put both liturgical renewal and ecclesial communion at risk. Likewise, in 1995, the bishops of Kansas issued a pastoral letter concerning 'Sunday Communion Without Mass', stating that they 'have come to judge that Holy Communion regularly received outside of Mass is a short-term solution that has all the makings of becoming a long-term problem'. The Church of England should take note that in the fourteen years since the *Directory on Sunday Celebrations in the Absence of a Priest* was published, Roman Catholics have seen an ongoing decline in the number of vocations; and despite grave concern, it seems their only solution remains lay-led Sunday worship with communion by extension.

In his commentary on *Public Worship with Communion by Extension*, Phillip Tovey makes a crucial point:

> '[The problem posed by communion by extension] entails some reconsideration of expectations about priesthood. It became a quasi-profession, with expectations of levels of training and reward. This is all changing. New methods of training have developed . . . New vision is developing. Churches need to "lift up their eyes" to the wider picture and not discuss Communion by Extension in order to keep the show on the road, but rather to see it as a temporary stage into a new world of local leadership.' [139]

Such thoughts may unnerve those who harbour a strong affection for familiar patterns of ministry; but they are undoubtedly pertinent. Of course we need not be under any illusion that fresh thinking about ministry is a straightforward

---

139 P Tovey, *Public Worship with Communion by Extension: A Commentary* (Grove Worship Series No.167, Grove Books Ltd, Cambridge, 2001) p 23.

task, or that new forms will emerge without false-starts and side-tracks; but some kind of development in this area is surely the appropriate response to prevailing pastoral circumstances. Once again, Tovey points to a possible way forward:

> 'My suggestion is that pastoral necessity [i.e. lack of priests] be always put in the context of local leadership. This would mean that on the application to the bishop a parish would set its argument for Communion by Extension in the context of the wider picture of the development of local ministry. Unless this sort of approach is included then Communion by Extension might in the long run do more harm than good.'[140]

If there is one contribution this study can make to the ongoing debate about ministry, it is to remind the Church that priests are ordained to serve the eucharist, not the other way round. In the end, the eucharist is Christ's action within the Church whereby we are united with his self-offering to the Father and become, by him and with him and in him, in the unity of the Holy Spirit, the body of Christ, to be sent out in loving service to the world. Take this away from the Church, and there is nothing left. The eucharist makes the Church—dare we dismantle it?

---

140 *Ibid.* p 23

Alcuin/GROW Joint Liturgical Studies

All cost £4.95 (US $8) in 2002—nos. 4 and 16 are out of print

1. (LS 49) **Daily and Weekly Worship—from Jewish to Christian** by Roger Beckwith
2. (LS 50) **The Canons of Hippolytus** edited by Paul Bradshaw
3. (LS 51) **Modern Anglican Ordination Rites** edited by Colin Buchanan
4. (LS 52) **Models of Liturgical Theology** by James Empereur
5. (LS 53) **A Kingdom of Priests: Liturgical Formation of the Laity: The Brixen Essays** edited by Thomas Talley
6. (LS 54) **The Bishop in Liturgy: an Anglican Study** edited by Colin Buchanan
7. (LS 55) **Inculturation: the Eucharist in Africa** by Phillip Tovey
8. (LS 56) **Essays in Early Eastern Initiation** edited by Paul Bradshaw,
9. (LS 57) **The Liturgy of the Church in Jerusalem** by John Baldovin
10. (LS 58) **Adult Initiation** edited by Donald Withey
11. (LS 59) **'The Missing Oblation': The Contents of the Early Antiochene Anaphora** by John Fenwick
12. (LS 60) **Calvin and Bullinger on the Lord's Supper** by Paul Rorem
13-14 (LS 61) **The Liturgical Portions of the Apostolic Constitutions: A Text for Students** edited by W. Jardine Grisbrooke (This double-size volume costs double price (i.e. £9.90))
15 (LS 62) **Liturgical Inculturation in the Anglican Communion** edited by David Holeton
16. (LS 63) **Cremation Today and Tomorrow** by Douglas Davies
17. (LS 64) **The Preaching Service—The Glory of the Methodists** by Adrian Burdon
18. (LS 65) **Irenaeus of Lyon on Baptism and Eucharist** edited with Introduction, Translation and Commentary by David Power
19. (LS 66) **Testamentum Domini** edited by Grant Sperry-White
20. (LS 67) **The Origins of the Roman Rite** edited by Gordon Jeanes
21. **The Anglican Eucharist in New Zealand 1814-1989** by Bosco Peters
22-23 **Foundations of Christian Music: The Music of Pre-Constantinian Christianity** by Edward Foley (double-sized volume at £9.90)
24. **Liturgical Presidency** by Paul James
25. **The Sacramentary of Sarapion of Thmuis: A Text for Students** edited by Ric Lennard-Barrett
26. **Communion Outside the Eucharist** by Phillip Tovey
27. **Revising the Eucharist: Groundwork for the Anglican Communion** edited by David Holeton
28. **Anglican Liturgical Inculturation in Africa** edited by David Gitari
29-30. **On Baptismal Fonts: Ancient and Modern** by Anita Stauffer (double-sized volume at £9.90)
31. **The Comparative Liturgy of Anton Baumstark** by Fritz West
32. **Worship and Evangelism in Pre-Christendom** by Alan Kreider
33. **Liturgy in Early Christian Egypt** by Maxwell E. Johnson
34. **Welcoming the Baptized** by Timothy Turner
35. **Daily Prayer in the Reformed Tradition: An Initial Survey** by Diane Karay Tripp
36. **The Ritual Kiss in Early Christian Worship** by Edward Phillips
37. **'After the Primitive Christians': The Eighteenth-century Anglican Eucharist in its Architectural Setting** by Peter Doll
38. **Coronations Past, Present and Future** edited by Paul Bradshaw
39. **Anglican Orders and Ordinations** edited by David Holeton
40. **The Liturgy of St James as presently used** edited by Phillip Tovey
41. **Anglican Missals** by Mark Dalby
42. **The Origins of the Roman Rite vol 2** edited by Gordon Jeanes
43. **Baptism in Early Byzantine Palestine 325-451** by Juliette Day
44. **Ambrosianum Mysterium: the Church of Milan and its Liturgical Tradition Vol. 1** by Cesare Alzati (translated by George Guiver)
45. **Mar Nestorius and Mar Theodore the Interpreter: the Forgotten Eucharistic Prayers of East Syria** edited by Bryan Spinks
46. **The Eucharistic Theology of the Later Nonjurors** by James Smith
47-48. **Ambrosianum Mysterium: the Church of Milan and its Liturgical Tradition Vol. II** by Cesare Alzati (translated by George Guiver) (double-sized volume at £9.90)
49. **The Syriac Version of the Liturgy of St James: A brief history for Students** by Dr Baby Varghese
50. **Offerings from Kenya to Anglicanism: Liturgical Texts and Contents including 'A Kenyan Service of Holy Communion'** by Graham Kings and Geoff Morgan
51. **Early Jewish Liturgy: A Source Book for use by Students of Early Christian Liturgy** edited and translated by Alistair Stewart-Sykes and Judith H Newman
52. **Church and Worship in Fifth-Century Rome: The Letter of Innocent I to Decentius of Gubbio** by Martin F Connell